COMBAT AIRCRAFT SERIES

CW01024548

F-14 Tomcat

LINDSAY PEACOCK

OSPREY PUBLISHING LONDON

Published in 1986 by
Osprey Publishing Ltd
Member Company of the George Philip Group
12–14 Long Acre, London WC2E 9LP

© Copyright 1986 Bedford Editions Ltd.

British Library Cataloguing in Publication Data

Peacock, Lindsay T.
    F-14 Tomcat.—(Osprey combat aircraft)
    1. Tomcat (Jet fighter plane)—History
    I. Title
    623.74′64   UG1242.F5

ISBN 0-85045-720-3

Typeset by Flair plan Photo-typesetting Ltd.
Printed by Proost International Book Production,
Turnhout, Belgium.

Colour artworks: © Pilot Press Ltd, and by Mike Keep
(© Salamander Books Ltd.)
Diagrams: TIGA.
Photographs: The publishers would like to thank
Grumman Aerospace Corp., and the US Department of
Defense for the photographs reproduced in this book.

The Author
LINDSAY PEACOCK is an aviation journalist and
photographer who has written extensively on
military aircraft subjects for books and magazines,
especially in areas of specific interest to aircraft
modellers. He has travelled widely in pursuit of his
profession and hobbies, and spent much time on
aircraft carrier decks observing his subjects at close
quarters. He is the author of another book in this
series, *F/A-18 Hornet*.

Contents

1
Evolution of the Tomcat

FINDING a replacement for the almost incredibly versatile McDonnell Douglas F-4 Phantom was never going to be easy although as far as the US Navy was concerned it was perhaps a slightly less complex matter than that faced by the Air Force.

Certainly, from the Navy's viewpoint, the basic task to be fulfilled by any new fighter type—that of fleet defence—must have simplified matters greatly, for this service had, historically, tended to pursue a "horses for courses" philosophy. Thus, when it came to procurement, Naval aircraft were almost invariably closely tailored for a specific mission, classic examples of this single-minded policy being the Grumman A-6 Intruder medium attack aircraft and the Chance Vought F-8 Crusader interceptor.

Whether this was the right policy to pursue is open to debate but it seems to have served the Navy well for many years, resulting in a succession of superlative combat aircraft which helped US naval aviation move from a position of being "a poor relation" when compared with the US Air Force to one of

qualitative parity. Types such as the Douglas A-4 Skyhawk, Ling-Temco-Vought A-7 Corsair and McDonnell Douglas F-4 Phantom were instrumental in this process, although it is interesting to note that the Navy has now also got into the "all-singing, all-dancing" act, its newest combat type being the McDonnell Douglas/Northrop F-18 Hornet which does possess genuine multi-mission capability.

That, however, is probably as much a result of economy as anything else, for the process of developing modern warplanes is what one can only describe as "cash-intensive". By opting for multi-mission machines, it is possible to curtail development costs and, eventually, to end up with more hardware than would otherwise have been the case had separate paths been pursued.

Altough the Navy now appears to support multi-mission capability, the machine chosen for the unenviable job of replacing the Phantom certainly cannot

Below: Depicted at Grumman's Calverton facility during the final stages of preparation for its maiden flight, F-14 prototype Bu.No.157980 was destined to enjoy only a brief career.

be considered a compromise, Grumman's F-14 Tomcat being conceived primarily to fulfil the various functions which combine to form the fleet defence mission. Admittedly, Tomcat does in theory possess secondary air-to-ground capability but this is limited at best, does not feature in the training syllabus and should more correctly be viewed as a latent capability. In view of that, Tomcat may well ultimately prove to be historically significant as the last dedicated fighter to be acquired by this service.

Alternative proposals

Although development of what eventually matured into the Tomcat was not formally authorized by the US Navy until the summer of 1968, Grumman's design bureaux had been actively exploring numerous alternative avenues since the mid-1960s. Impetus for this design effort was provided by the less than satisfactory progress being made by the General Dynamics/Grumman F-111B. Collectively known as Project 303, the best of more than 6,000 configurations were presented to senior Navy personnel in 1967 but with the F-111B still expected to be the next carrier-borne fighter there was little that the service could do, although it did set up a study group to consider the merits and demerits of Grumman's work.

Plagued by a host of problems—not least of which was unacceptably high weight and, ironically in view of the Tomcat's later experiences, difficulties with the

Above: The large trailing edge flaps and leading edge slats are readily apparent in this study of the F-14A Tomcat second prototype (Bu.No.157981) at Calverton in 1971.

TF30 engines—the navalized F-111B eventually fell victim to cancellation in December 1968 although in truth the project had effectively been killed off in May of that year when Congress blocked further funding.

Although the loss of the F-111B apparently left the Navy with nothing to show for ten years of work, cancellation of this type eventually proved advantageous, for it opened the way for procurement of a new "custom-built" machine to equip Navy fighter squadrons. Not surprisingly, the service wasted little time in setting about this task, issuing a formal Request for Proposals (RFP) to industry in July 1968, at about the same moment as work on the F-111B terminated due to funding starvation.

Known as VFX (Heavier-than-air Fighter, Experimental), the requirement stipulated that any proposal should be for a tandem two-seat twin-engined aircraft incorporating an advanced weapon control system, sophisticated missile armament including either the AIM-54 Phoenix or a mix of AIM-7 Sparrows and AIM-9 Sidewinders plus an integral Vulcan M61A 20-mm cannon.

The response from industry was immediate and enthusiastic, no fewer than five companies taking part in the battle for this potentially lucrative contract. Naturally, in the light of its continuing design studies, Grumman was one contender, the others

Above: With wings swept at differing angles, three of the dozen research, development, test and evaluation Tomcats fly in formation above a densely populated part of Long Island.

being General Dynamics, Ling-Temco-Vought, McDonnell Douglas and North American Rockwell. By the year-end, Grumman and McDonnell Douglas were being viewed as "favourites" to secure the development award.

Even as work on the ill-fated F-111B was winding down to its unhappy conclusion, Grumman had been busily firming up Project 303 and was not slow to

Below: Liberally covered in high-visibility red paint, the fifth example of the Tomcat receives fuel from a US Marine Corps Lockeed KC-130F Hercules tanker during 1971.

respond to the RFP, submitting a variant based on the Model 303E study for consideration. On 14 January 1969, this was selected as the winning design, Grumman being awarded a contract covering the construction of six research, development, test and evaluation (RDT&E) aircraft and no fewer than 463 production examples for service with both the US Navy and US Marine Corps. Eventually, procurement was expected to exceed the 700 mark.

Project 303 gets a name

At the same time, the designation F-14 was allocated to the new fighter, it being intended to begin production with a fairly limited number of F-14As before switching to the definitive F-14B model. The six RDT&E examples plus the first 61 production specimens would all be F-14As powered by Pratt & Whitney's TF30-P-412, subsequent machines being fitted with the new advanced technology engine (ATE) which was then under development and expected to become available in about 1973. Aircraft with the ATE would be known as F-14Bs although, in the event, it didn't quite work out like that.

In its original form, the F-14 would have featured a single vertical tail, folding ventral fins on the outer surfaces of each aft engine bay being fitted to provide good directional stability. Eventually, though, the Navy objected to this layout, largely on the grounds that it would not be suitable for carrier operations. Deletion of the ventral fins in turn led to the possibility that a single vertical tail might not be able to bestow sufficient directional stability in the event of engine failure at high Mach with the result that it was decided to adopt a twin-fin layout similar to that employed by the MiG-25 Foxbat, one of the "threats" that the new Grumman fighter would be called upon to counter.

Despite the fact that the newest "cat" to emerge from the "Iron Works" would be far and away the most sophisticated and complex design thus far produced by that company, the period of time which elapsed between contract award and first flight was remarkably short. Indeed, one of the stipulations laid down by the contract concerned the maiden flight, it being specified that this take place within two years, on or before 31 January 1971 to be precise.

That this target date was met was probably due in no small part to that fact that Grumman was highly confident that it would be selected to build the Navy's next fighter. This confidence was perhaps best exemplified by the decision to initiate fabrication of certain components shortly before the end of 1968 and some weeks in advance of contract award. This prompt start eventually enabled Grumman to begin taxi trials with the first development aircraft (Bu.No.157980) on 14 December 1970 but it was to be another week before this aircraft got airborne for what proved to be an uneventful maiden flight for Grumman Chief Test Pilot Robert Smythe and Project Test Pilot William Miller on 21 December.

Loss of Tomcat No. 1

Nine days later, the term "crash programme" took on literal as well as metaphorical meaning when this valuable prototype was lost during only its second sortie. On the day in question—30 December 1970—the same pilots were in command, and early test objectives included stability and control assessment

Below: With sunlight reflecting from its port fin, F-14A Bu.No.158625 of the Pacific Missile Test Center at Point Mugu carries a dummy AMRAAM beneath the forward fuselage.

with the landing gear down. Then the aircraft was "cleaned up" and the speed allowed to increase steadily to a peak of 180kt (332km/h). Clearly, Smythe and Miller were determined to "make haste slowly" but their caution was to no avail, one of the chase aircraft reporting that smoke appeared to be coming from the F-14 some 25 minutes into the mission.

At the same moment, Miller—who was in command on this occasion—reported that the primary hydraulic system had failed, the "smoke" actually being hydraulic fluid pouring from ruptured tubing. Switching to the back-up flight system, Miller began to nurse the Tomcat back to Calverton, lowering the undercarriage at a distance of four miles (6km) from the field and raising hopes that it would be possible to save the prototype.

Unfortunately, the flight hydraulic system also

Below: Rescued from relative obscurity, the sole F-14B prototype (Bu.No.157986) was used to flight-test the F101DFE turbofan in 1981, being referred to as the Super Tomcat by Grumman.

chose this moment to fail. Miller then turned to the Combat Survival System which, although mainly intended to provide a measure of control so as to permit battle-damaged aircraft to get clear of the combat zone before the crew ejected, seemed to offer a chance of completing a safe landing. In the event, with the runway just seconds away, Miller realised that he was no longer in control and, rather than continue to fight a losing battle, elected to eject. Both pilots escaped safely, although they came down perilously close to the fireball which erupted when the Tomcat impacted just a mile (1.6km) short of the runway.

Subsequent investigation pinpointed the cause as being resonance-induced fracture of the titanium hydraulic lines, a failure compounded by a loose mounting connection. The fix was simple, stainless steel being adopted in lieu of titanium on ensuing test and production Tomcats. Inevitably, though, this accident led to some delay and it was not until 24 May 1971 that flight testing resumed, with the second RDT&E aircraft making its maiden flight.

Once again, Smythe and Miller were in charge and the 58-minute sortie passed off entirely uneventfully, as did a two-hour trip a couple of days later. By this time, however, the number of aircraft earmarked to fulfil RDT&E functions had been doubled. These were entrusted with the lion's share of test duty although a similar number of early production-configured F-14As also made a valuable contribution, especially during the later stages which included weapons-related testing under near-operational conditions similar to those likely to be encountered when the Tomcat entered service with Fleet units.

As was usual Navy practice, various aspects of the test effort were undertaken from various bases. The Naval Air Test Center (NATC) was probably the most important single agency during the entire programme for it was this that was responsible for overseeing major milestones in the Navy's formal assessment process. Unusually, though, a considerable amount of test flying was conducted from Grumman's own facility at Calverton. This was largely brought about by the desire to take full advantage of the Automated Telemetry System (ATS) located there.

An extremely sophisticated piece of kit, ATS permitted multiple test objectives to be accomplished in a single sortie and eliminated the need for aircraft to

Above: The first of two aircraft earmarked to serve as F-14B prototypes, Bu.No.157986 was eventually the only one to appear. It has spent much of its life in store at Calverton.

return to base so as to permit data to be retrieved for analysis by the test team. In-flight refuelling, accomplished by a trio of A-6 Intruder tankers, also enabled the F-14 test aircraft to spend more time aloft than would normally be the case and this too was of great value in accelerating the rate of progress, although it should be emphasised that the often hectic pace was not achieved at the cost of flight safety.

Typical of the formal hurdles which had to be be negotiated was NPE 1 (Navy Preliminary Evaluation One) which was conducted in December 1971 and which was mainly concerned with verification of the flight envelope. NPE 2—completed in July and August 1972—was rather more comprehensive, involving four aircraft and two major test centres. Personnel from NATC Patuxent River went to Calverton to assess handling qualities in a variety of armed configurations whilst the Naval Missile Center at Point Mugu (later renamed the Pacific Missile Test Center) examined the Hughes AWG-9 weapons control system and other key items of avionics equipment.

Then, in the autumn of 1973, the final hurdle prior to full-scale fleet introduction was successfully cleared, this being the Board of Inspection and Survey (BIS) trials programme. An exhaustive examination of all aspects of the aircraft, BIS can perhaps be likened to the certification process which all commercial airliners have to undergo before being cleared to carry fare-paying passengers. In truth, though, BIS is probably rather more complex since it also has to take into account such aspects as the fire control system and its associated weaponry, deck handling qualities, launch and recovery characteristics and basic performance.

Naturally, some of these criteria are highly specialized disciplines and it is usual for various elements of the BIS trials to be accomplished by specialist test agencies. Thus, personnel assigned to NATC's Service Test Division and Weapons Systems Test Division were closely involved, as were those from the NMC at Point Mugu, while the Naval Weapons Center (NWC) at China Lake and the Naval Weapons Laboratory at Dahlgren may also have furnished specialists for some aspects of BIS trials.

Despite the fact that successful completion of BIS assessment is imperative if an aircraft is to go on to a fully-fledged naval career, it really only marks the end of the beginning for there is still much to be done before any new type takes its place aboard a Navy aircraft carrier. In the case of the Tomcat, although this phase of test work was completed in the autumn of 1973, almost another year was to pass before the type deployed with the US Navy in an operational capacity. The distinction of being the first units to take Grumman's potent new fighter to sea was shared by VF-1 "Wolf Pack" and VF-2 "Bounty Hunters" which duly departed from the US West Coast port of Alameda, California, aboard the nuclear-powered aircraft carrier USS *Enterprise* (CVAN-65) during September 1974. Operating as part of Carrier Air Wing 14 (CVW-14), they spent the next six months at sea in a deployment which had its high points but which was marred by the loss of two aircraft, these being among the first Tomcats to fall victim to the engine-related problems which were to cause so many headaches for everyone associated with the F-14 programme.

2
Building the Tomcat

GRUMMAN has, of course, a long and illust-rious history of producing fine carrier-borne fighters, which have, for the most part, married good performance with immense strength. The latest cat to claw its way off the Grumman design boards certainly lives up to those traditions, for the F-14 epitomises all that is best about Grumman fighters, being incredibly strong while also possessing handling and performance qualities which make it more than a match for most of its likely opponents. The F-14D variant will be an even more potent and deadly adversary and there is no doubt that the Tomcat will still form an important part of the Navy's sea-going arsenal at the end of the present century, almost 30 years after it first entered service.

Grumman's Calverton facility on Long Island is where Tomcat finally comes together, the process of manufacture actually being undertaken at several widely separated locations and by a number of different companies, sub-contracting playing a major part in the overall programme. Eventually, though, all of the various strands converge on Calverton and, more specifically, Plant 6 which serves as the assem-bly hall not only for Tomcat but also for the Intruder and Prowler.

Modular assembly concept

Assembly of the F-14 centres around the use of a modular concept, seven stations being intimately associated, and each is responsible for different aspects of this process. Station A is the starting point for it is here that mating of the nacelle assembly to the forward/centre-fuselage module, mating of the aft fuselage and nacelle assemblies and fitting of the inlet/glove assemblies and cockpit canopy take place. Moving on to Station One, what will eventually emerge as Tomcat begins to take on recognizable shape, the vertical tail surface and main undercar-

riage members being added, fitment of the latter permitting the aircraft to move freely on its own wheels throughout the remainder of the manufac-turing stage.

Wings and engines are added to the F-14 at Station Two, while rigging and testing of flight control systems takes place at Station Three, the latter also being responsible for installing the Hughes AN/AWG-9 Weapons Control System, Central Air Data Computer (CADC) and other mission-related avionics. Check-out of avionics equipment occurs at Station Four, the virtually complete aircraft then moving outside to Station Five for engine testing and fuel flow system calibration before going to Station Six for painting, Tomcat originally conforming to the standard US Navy gull grey and white colour scheme.

More recently, the trend of adopting low visibility markings has witnessed a change to a scheme em-

Below: Some idea of the complexity of the Tomcat's structure can be gleaned from this view of an early F-14A undergoing final assembly at Calverton. Comparison of this with later pictures also reveals how the boat tail section between the twin fins has changed since the Tomcat first flew in 1970.

ploying varying shades of grey in conjunction with toned-down unit insignia, the latter being applied once the aircraft reaches its assigned squadron.

The final stages of preparation take place at Plant Seven where weapons racks are added and where the weapons system is subjected to further checks, this process including gun-firing tests. Only then is the aircraft cleared for flight, Grumman test pilots taking it aloft for the first time and giving it a fairly thorough work-out before turning it over to the Navy's Calverton-based acceptance team which also flies each F-14 before it is considered ready for despatch to a Fleet unit at either Miramar, California or Oceana, Virginia.

First use of beam welding

Construction is largely conventional with perhaps the most important structure being the single-cell titanium box beam, this being of particular interest in that it is the first major application of electron beam welding in the manufacture of a modern combat aircraft. Fabricated from no less than 33 machined parts, the 22-foot long (6.7m) box transmits wing loadings to the fuselage via two sets of wing pivots and also serves as an integral fuel tank. Attachment to the fuselage is accomplished by just four pin joints. Wing pivots comprise a brace of annular, spherical bearings, made up largely of titanium alloy with

Below: Part of the mind-boggling wiring which is contained in every F-14 is clearly evident in this view of a Tomcat taking shape at Grumman's Calverton facility.

Teflon-type surfaces. Bolts are employed for attachment to the wing box.

Turning to the fuselage, this is assembled around machined frames, steel being used for the aft fuselage and undercarriage support frame as well as for the spectacle beam on which the rear engine and stabiliser mounts are situated. Bonded honeycomb panels are extensively used for fuselage skinning although the aft "hot section" adjacent to the engines utilises titanium which is better able to withstand the high temperatures found in this area while also having the advantage of being highly resistant to corrosion, always welcome in the maritime environment. Titanium is also used for upper and lower wing skins, a hot forming moulding process enabling the desired amount of curvature to be obtained without too much wastage.

Bonded honeycomb material is also used for the glove vanes in the wing leading edge adjacent to the air intakes, for the inlet duct sidewalls, for leading and trailing edges of the wing and, finally, for the movable control surfaces. The twin fins make use of honeycomb sandwich skinning while the horizontal tail surfaces, or "tailerons" as they are perhaps better known, represented a unique feature when the F-14 entered service, these being the very first instance of composite materials being used for load-bearing applications on any Western production aircraft, the skins actually being made up of boron-epoxy. Conversely, titanium is used for the engine intakes, hydraulic lines, main and aft fuselage longerons and engine support beam.

Power behind the Tomcat

At the time of the Tomcat's debut, it was powered by a pair of Pratt & Whitney TF30-P-412 turbofan engines, a variant which very quickly gave way to the TF30-P-412A which was rated at a maximum of 20,900lbs (9,480kg) thrust in afterburner. Housed in widely separated "pods" on each side of the fuselage, air is fed to the engines via two-dimensional air intakes situated well in advance of wing flow fields, while the positioning of the intakes 7in (17.8cm) outboard of the fuselage prevents the ingestion of sluggish boundary layer air and obviates the requirement for splitter plates.

Air flowing through the intakes is compressed by forward-facing variable-position ramps which over-

collapse so as to offer additional area during take-off and landing, thus doing away with the need for suck-in doors or hinged cowls. A throat-bleed slot is employed to disperse boundary layer air via doors on the upper wing surface, the remaining air being compressed in a subsonic diffuser duct before passing to the face of the engine. Operation of intake deflection ramps is accomplished automatically by the Central Air Data Computer (CADC) as a function of Mach number while the dual-position throat-bleed door operates at high angles of attack (AOA) to inhibit the possibility of engine stall problems—a failing which it does not appear to have completely overcome—or at high speed to prevent "buzz". Jet efflux nozzles are of the so-called convergent/divergent (con/di) type, this being considered as most suitable for critical subsonic conditions. In addition to possessing a lower installed weight, the con/di nozzles are apparently superior to other types in the speed range encompassing Mach 1.5 to Mach 2.0.

It is common knowledge that the TF30 engine was directly responsible for quite a few instances of

Above: Unarmed save for a single AIM-9 Sidewinder apiece, two F-14A Tomcats sweep low over the USS *Saratoga* during flight operations in the Mediterranean during January 1986.

attrition during the first few years of F-14 operation but it was not until the 235th Tomcat was delivered that a new variant of the turbofan became available. Given the designation TF30-P-414, this was partly conceived to address the fan blade failures which had claimed a few victims, disintegrating blades tending to scythe through anything that got in their way when they parted company with the turbine, usually with quite disastrous results.

The most notable change evident on the 'dash 414 model entailed steel containment cases being fitted around the first three fan stages as a kind of "damage control" measure in the event of blades being "thrown" by the rapidly revolving turbine. At the same time, slightly different materials were employed in fan blade manufacture, while some atten-

Below: Carrying a quartet of Sidewinders and two AIM-7 Sparrows, a VF-103 F-14A trails its arrester hook in anticipation of recovery aboard the USS *Saratoga*.

GRUMMAN F-14A TOMCAT CUTAWAY

1. Pressure sensor.
2. Radar target horn.
3. Radome.
4. Flight refuelling probe.
5. ADF sense aerial.
6. Windscreen rain dispersal air ducts.
7. Incidence probe.
8. Rudder pedals.
9. Pilot's instrument displays.
10. Head-up display.
11. Control column.
12. Wing sweep control.
13. Throttle levers.
14. Pilot's Martin-Baker "zero-zero" ejection seat.
15. Naval Flight Officer's instrument console.
16. "Kick-in" boarding step.
17. Radar hand controller.
18. Cockpit canopy cover.
19. Naval Flight Officer's ejection seat.
20. Canopy jack.
21. Glove vane hydraulic jack.
22. Starboard glove vane.
23. Navigation light.
24. UHF/TACAN aerial.
25. Forward fuselage fuel tanks.
26. Intake spill door and hydraulic jack.
27. Leading edge slat.
28. Starboard wing integral fuel tank.

29. Starboard navigation light.
30. Formation light.
31. Spoilers.
32. Outboard manoeuvre flaps.
33. Flap sealing vane.
34. Wing pivot box integral fuel tank.
35. Inboard high-lift flap.
36. Manoeuvre flap and slat drive motor and gearbox.
37. Emergency hydraulic generator.
38. UHF/IFF aerial.
39. Wing sweep actuating screw jack.
40. Inflatable wing seal.
41. Engine bleed air ducting.
42. Flight control rod linkages.
43. Wing fully swept position.
44. Wing "overswept" position (carrier storage).
45. Aft fuselage fuel tanks.
46. Starboard all-moving tailplane.
47. Rudder hydraulic actuator.
48. Airbrake hydraulic jack.
49. Airbrake, above and below.
50. Tail navigation light.
51. ECM aerial.
52. Starboard rudder.
53. Fully variable convergent/divergent afterburner nozzle.
54. Anti-collision light.
55. Formation lighting strip.

56. ECM aerial.
57. Port rudder.
58. Fuel jettison.
59. ECM aerial.
60. Deck arrester hook.
61. Chaff and flare dispensers.
62. Afterburner nozzle control jacks.
63. Radar warning receiver.
64. Port all-moving tailplane.
65. Tailplane pivot bearing.
66. Tailplane hydraulic actuator.

67. Arrester hook dashpot.
68. Pratt & Whitney TF30-P-412 afterburning turbofan engines.
69. Formation lighting strip.
70. Hydraulic system filters.
71. Oil cooler air intake.
72. Formation light.
73. Port navigation light.
74. Manoeuvre flap rotary actuators and pushrods.
75. Port leading edge slat.

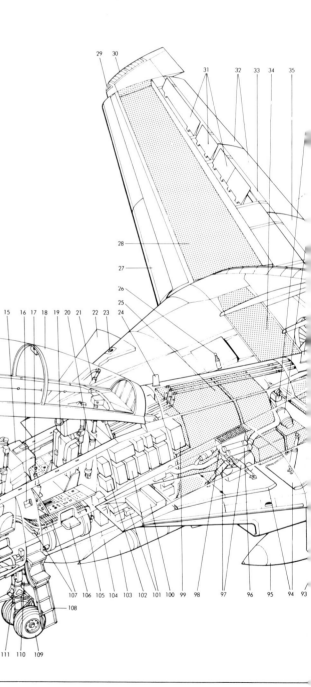

76. Port wing integral fuel tank.
77. Spoiler hydraulic actuators.
78. Slat drive shaft.
79. Flap drive shaft.
80. Slat rotary actuators and guide rails.
81. Hydraulic reservoir.
82. Engine accessory equipment gearbox.
83. Inboard flap hydraulic jack.

84. Main undercarriage hydraulic retraction jack.
85. Undercarriage leg pivot bearing.
86. Forward retracting mainwheel.
87. Wing pivot bearing.
88. Sparrow missile adaptor.
89. AIM-7 Sparrow air-to-air missile.
90. Wing glove pylon.
91. AIM-9 Sidewinder air-to-air missile.

92. Flap and slat bevel drive gearbox.
93. Telescopic drive shaft.
94. Variable area intake ramps.
95. External fuel tank.
96. Hydraulic brake accumulators
97. Intake ramp hydraulic actuators.
98. Air conditioning system heat exchanger.
99. Air data computer.
100. Electrical relay panel.

101. Avionics equipment bays.
102. Electrical system equipment.
103. AIM-54A Phoenix air-to-air missile (4).
104. Phoenix missile pallet.
105. Ammunition drum.
106. Boarding step.
107. Ammunition feed and link return chutes.
108. Boarding ladder.
109. Forward retracting nosewheels.
110. Nosewheel steering actuator.
111. Carrier approach lights.
112. Catapult launch strop.
113. M-61-A1 20mm six barrel rotary cannon.
114. Canopy emergency release.
115. Pitot head.
116. Formation lighting strips.
117. Radar equipment bay.
118. ECM antenna.
119. AWG-9 pulse doppler flat plate radar scanner.

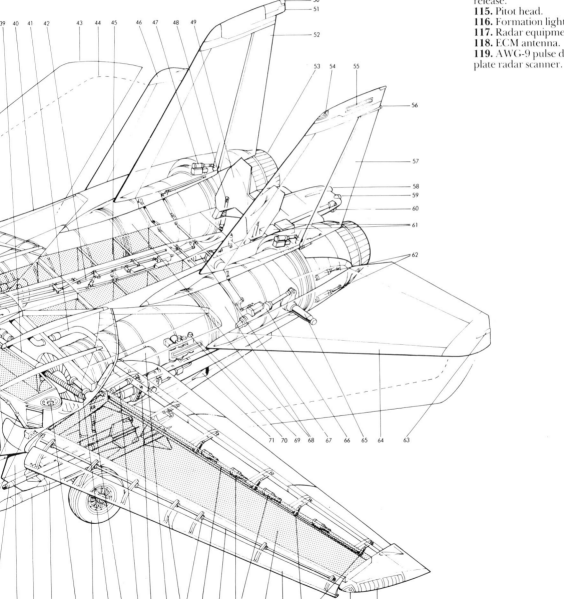

Above: In an interesting illustration of the convergent-divergent nozzle technology at work, this VF-74 Tomcat reveals the different configurations required by different power settings. The nozzle at left is in the typical idle position while that at right is fully open for maximum power output.

tion was also paid to fire prevention, titanium sheeting and ablative substances giving added protection in the event of fire. The switch to the TF30-P-414 also encompassed those aircraft which had already been delivered, retrospective modification being accomplished as the early Tomcats came in for depot level maintenance and, as a result, it was not until the summer of 1979 that the last 'dash 412 engine disappeared. By then it was apparent that, although the newer model was better, it still left a great deal to be desired, especially with regard to durability.

In view of that, it is hardly surprising that further "tweaking" of the 'dash 414 followed, culminating in the advent of the TF30-P-414A in the latter half of 1982 and this is now the standard engine on Tomcat. Offering increased mean time between overhaul, it is generally more reliable and has demonstrated greater resistance to compressor stall although the latter aspect is still a cause for very real concern today, more than a decade after the F-14 entered service.

Moving on to the variable geometry wing, control of the sweep angle is achieved automatically as a function of Mach and altitude, responsibility for managing this being entrusted to the Mach sweep programmer. For flight operations, sweep may vary from 20deg to 68deg measured at the wing leading edge, while for stowage in the cramped confines so prevalent at sea a 75deg oversweep facility exists.

While on the subject of flying surfaces, one particularly notable feature of the F-14 is the glove vane fitted to the leading edge of each fixed centre wing section. Operation of these is entrusted to the pilot and they may be used in either subsonic or supersonic flight. In the former instance, they can extend with slats and flaps to enhance lift during manoeuvring flight such as might be encountered in a dogfight

situation. Extension of the glove vanes is, however, restricted to just 5deg with the wings fully-spread, rising to a maximum of 15deg at sweep angles of 35deg and above. In supersonic flight, manual extension is possible at speeds of up to Mach 1.4. Once that point is reached the inevitable computer takes over responsibility for management. Maximum glove vane extension is reached at Mach 1.5 and these then remain fully open, one noteworthy benefit being that they alleviate forces on the horizontal tailplanes when flying at high speed, acting in much the same way as the canard surfaces do on the Swedish Viggen.

With regard to control surfaces and lift-augmenting devices, Tomcat is quite well endowed. Flaps are of the conventional single-slotted trailing edge type, three sections being fitted on each outer

wing panel. These consist of two outer main segments and one inner auxiliary segment, the latter becoming inoperative at sweep angles exceeding 22deg so as to eliminate the possibility of damage to the wing gloves. Similarly, operation of the main flap sections is inhibited when 50deg of wing sweep is reached.

In conjunction with conventional leading edge slats, this flap arrangement was felt to offer the best lift-generating characteristics when operating at low speed. However, in subsonic and transonic flight, the outer sections may double as manoeuvring flaps. Control rests with the CADC and this arrangement offers advantages in combat by delaying buffet and flow separation when operating at high load factors. With effect from the 185th Tomcat, hydraulically-actuated manoeuvring slats were provided to alleviate the buffet problem in, for instance, air combat manoeuvring training. Once again, these also operate as a function of Mach number.

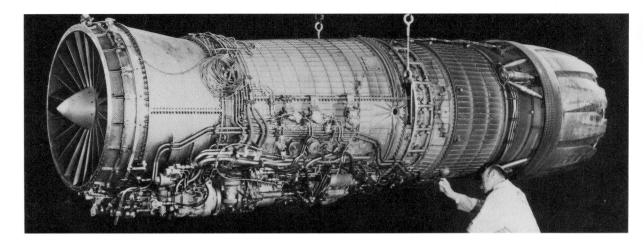

The twin fins of the F-14 provide an effective means of countering de-stabilising flow generated by the air intakes during sustained flight at high angles of attack while twin rudders are also provided. One less obvious benefit bestowed by Tomcat's empennage is that it resulted in lower overall height, thus making it compatible with hangar deck clearance and obviating the need for a folding fin similar to that used by the Vigilante. Horizontal tail surfaces or "tailerons" are of the fully-variable "flying" type, operating in unison to provide control in pitch and differentially for roll control. Not surprisingly, no ailerons are fitted.

Other control surfaces comprise spoilers and air brakes. As far as the former are concerned, independent pairs are located on the upper surface of each outer wing panel. Since an increase in the angle of sweep inevitably has a deleterious effect on spoiler performance, a series of mechanical locks come into play at 62deg of sweep so as to prevent inadvertent operation of the spoilers. Finally, Tomcat has two air brakes—positioned on the upper and lower fuselage boat tail surfaces between the engine exhaust nozzles—maximum deflection of that on the undersides being restricted when the undercarriage is lowered to provide adequate ground clearance.

On the hydraulic front, the F-14 has two main systems as well as an emergency back-up system providing a measure of pitch and yaw control. Thus, any crew unfortunate enough to lose the primary systems should be able to return to base and land safely. Finally, electrical power is furnished by a brace of 60/75 KVA generators, each of which is capable of providing sufficient current to operate all of the Tomcat's many systems. Once again, though, an emergency supply is available, this comprising a hydraulically-driven 5KVA generator which will enable a crew to get home safely.

3
Avionics and Armament

ANY FIGHTER is only as good as the weapons it carries. A sweeping statement, perhaps, and one that may well be hotly debated but, when everything else is taken into account, it is the armament which actually inflicts damage on an opponent. The aircraft's performance, or lack of it, obviously has an important part to play in air combat, for the fighter pilot has first to manoeuvre into a position of advantage. Aircrew skill is also a vital consideration, highly-trained pilots inevitably standing a far better chance of achieving success and, perhaps more importantly, of surviving to fly and fight again on another day. Without adequate weaponry, though, even the most skilled aircrew in the hottest fighter will be able to accomplish little.

In terms of armament, Tomcat is indeed fortunate, since the three types of missile that it can carry bestow the ability to engage opponents at short,

medium and long range with a high probability of killing them, while for close-in manoeuvring engagements—the traditional "dog-fight" although, in this instance, "cat-fight" would seem a more appropriate term—it carries a single example of the well-proven Vulcan M61A1 20-mm Gatling-type rotary cannon complete with 675 rounds of ammunition. This multiplicity of weapons means that the F-14 is arguably the best fighter flying in the world today: on the one hand, it has the ability to kill an opponent at extreme range and long before it can itself be threatened with destruction, while it may also look after itself in a dog-fight situation, perhaps the most demanding test of all in air warfare.

Ideally, of course, it is desirable to knock down enemy aircraft at great range, before they threaten

Below: Live firing exercises with the costly AIM-54 Phoenix missile are relatively rare occurrences, but here a VF-154 crew takes advantage of one such opportunity with a text-book launch.

either the F-14 itself or the Carrier Battle Group it is protecting. In this task—the so-called Barrier Combat Air Patrol or BarCAP—the Tomcat will operate at some considerable distance from the parent aircraft carrier, thus setting up a "fighter screen" that an enemy will have to penetrate if he is to stand any chance of inflicting serious damage.

AIM-54 Phoenix missile

When operating in the BarCAP role—as, indeed, in any function—F-14 armament may vary but it's a fairly safe bet that the long-range Hughes AIM-54 Phoenix would feature strongly. The maximum number of Phoenix missiles that can be carried is six—four in the "tunnel" between the widely-separated engines and two on underwing pylons that can also take a brace of shoulder-mounted AIM-9 Sidewinders. In practice, a more likely load would be four Phoenix, two Sparrows and two Sidewinders; this, in conjunction with the gun, would permit Tomcat to counter threats across a broad spectrum.

One of the most remarkable weapons to be developed in recent years, Phoenix is in fact a legacy of the ill-fated F-111B project, providing proof that not

everything about the F-111B was a total disaster nor that everything associated with it was simply junked when the flow of funds dried up. In fact, evolution of the Phoenix predated even that of the F-111B, a concept being drawn up as early as 1960 although it was not until August 1962 that the Hughes Aircraft Company was awarded a development contract.

Flight trials got under way during 1965, early testing revealing that the AIM-54 possessed considerable potential. Cancellation of the F-111B cast a shadow over the missile but does not seem to have put it at serious risk for it was very quickly selected to form part of the armament of the Navy's newest fighter project. Testing—largely accomplished under Naval Missile Center auspices at Point Mugu—occupied the remainder of the decade and eventually culminated in a production order being placed just before the end of 1970.

The initial version was the AIM-54A which became operational coincident with the introduction of Tomcat in the first half of the 1970s and which is still

Below: Although viewed mainly as an interceptor, Tomcat can operate with air-to-ground weapons and some idea of the variety of ordnance which may be carried can be gained from this view of a PMTC aircraft at Point Mugu. It is interesting to note that, apart from AAMs, no "smart" weapons are displayed.

in service today although production ceased in 1981 by which time more than 2,500 copies had been completed. Manufacture of a second variant, the AIM-54B, began shortly before the end of 1977, this being essentially similar though somewhat simpler in that it featured sheet-metal wings and fins in place of the honeycomb structure employed by the AIM-54A. Other changes were aimed at enhancing reliability and included all-digital guidance equipment as well as non-liquid environmental conditioning and hydraulic systems. More recently, the AIM-54C, a much improved version, has been introduced to fleet service and production of this Phoenix sub-type is continuing, the US Navy having announced that it eventually plans to procure no fewer than 3,467 AIM-54Cs at a cost which seems certain to exceed $4 billion.

Development of the AIM-54C was initiated at company expense in the autumn of 1976, test specimens becoming available some three years later with live firing trials getting under way at the beginning of June 1980. Once again, the principal objective was to improve reliability but the changes made on the AIM-54C were rather more extensive, it being what might well be called a true "second-generation" member of the Phoenix family in that it is more resistant to electronic countermeasures (ECM) and has superior performance to its predecessors. Extensive use of digital systems has resulted in greater accuracy and range while "kill probability" is enhanced through the adoption of a new Motorola target detection device, this detonating the warhead at the optimum moment to inflict maximum damage.

Poor quality control

About the only cloud on the horizon has been poor quality control, a problem that became apparent in summer 1984 when the Navy temporarily suspended acceptance of the weapon and one which probably stemmed from Hughes' having rapidly to expand the size of its work-force to meet demand not only for Phoenix but also for the AIM-120, a newer weapon which will eventually replace Sparrow as the primary medium-range missile on USAF, US Navy and US Marine Corps fighter aircraft. The Navy is

Below: Posing belly-up for the benefit of the camera, this VF-32 F-14A rather unusually totes a maximum "bag" of Phoenix missiles. A more normal weapons fit would comprise four AIM-54As, two AIM-7 Sparrows and two AIM-9 Sidewinders, which, with the gun, would enable all "threats" to be countered.

Above: The upward-hingeing nose radome and scanner dish of the Hughes AWG-9 weapons control system overshadow a YAIM-54A development copy of the Phoenix long-range AAM.

pressing on with plans to develop a second manufacturing source for the Phoenix by the end of the present decade, although it has been stressed that this is not attributable to the deficiencies which began to manifest themselves in 1984.

Despite these problems, Phoenix is without doubt an outstanding weapon, having demonstrated its potential against a variety of targets operating at high, medium and low altitude and simulating many of the threats it will be expected to counter. Many of these tests have been well documented but among the more spectacular was one in April 1973 when a single missile was launched against a BQM-34E Firebee drone flying at Mach 1.5 and simulating a Backfire-type target at a distance of 110nm (204km). Just over two-and-a-half minutes later, the AIM-54 passed within lethal distance of the drone target, which, remarkably, was still more than 70 miles (112.6km) from the launch point. Seven months later, in November, an even more ambitious trial was staged, one Tomcat using six Phoenix to engage half-a-dozen drone targets flying at medium altitude at speeds varying from Mach 0.6 to Mach 1.1. Three direct hits and one lethal near-miss ensued, one missile failing and one being later declared a "no-test" due to a drone malfunction.

All variants of the Phoenix require that the target be illuminated by the F-14's on-board AWG-9 weapon system during intitial and mid-course phases of flight. During the terminal homing stage, however, the AIM-54's own radar takes over, this apparently having an effective range of about 10nm (18.5km).

Tomcat's current medium-range weapon—the AIM-7 Sparrow—is rather less self-supportive in that

Above: Complete with practice round, a Phoenix missile "shoe" is manoeuvred into position on the Tomcat mock-up during weapons compatibility tests at Calverton.

Below: The only item of armament "built-in" to the F-14A is the Gatling-type M61A1 20mm rotary cannon, a six-barrelled weapon which comes complete with 675 rounds of ammunition.

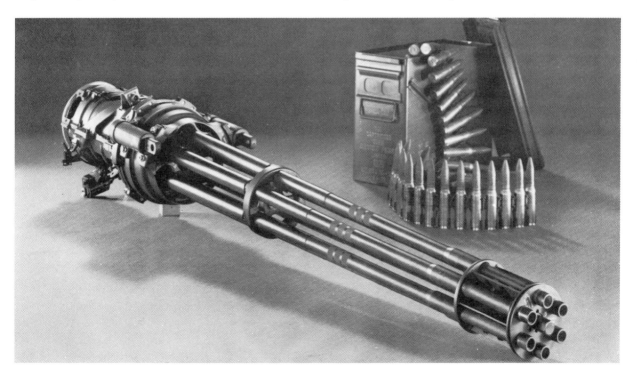

it requires a target to be continually "painted" by AWG-9 if it is to stand any chance of homing accurately. When the F-14A first entered service, the AIM-7E was the principal Sparrow model but this has since been supplanted by the more capable AIM-7F and AIM-7M, the latter being the current production version. Eventually, though, Sparrow will give way to the Hughes AIM-120A Advanced Medium-Range Air-to-Air Missile (AMRAAM), a considerably more sophisticated weapon and one that possesses its own active radar seeker operating in the X-band. Thus, unlike Sparrow, it will not be dependent on the launch aircraft once it has left the missile rail, being what is usually referred to as a "fire-and-forget" weapon and one that will permit multiple targets to be engaged in the medium-range area. Dimensionally similar to Sparrow, AIM-120 will be compatible with existing stores stations which can accommodate a maximum of six AIM-7s.

The successful Sidewinder

Tomcat's third missile is the tried and tested Sidewinder, an infra-red homing weapon that entered production as long ago as the mid-1950s and one which has been progressively refined ever since. The latest variant of this most successful missile is the AIM-9M which entered production in 1981 and which, like the AIM-9L that achieved such great success in the Falklands War, is a true "all-aspect" version, possessing a seeker head capable of homing

on skin friction. It can therefore be used with a measure of confidence against approaching targets, for, even if it does not succeed in destroying them, there is every chance that it could cause them to commit a tactical error and perhaps manoeuvre into a vulnerable position. Tomcat can carry up to four AIM-9s underwing although, as noted earlier, a more normal load would be two in conjunction with two Sparrow and four Phoenix.

Tomcat's 20mm cannon

Finally, of course, there is the integral gun which is very much in vogue again, largely as a result of combat experience gained in Vietnam where it soon became apparent that cannon armament was quite a useful piece of kit, not only for air-to-ground strafing but also for air-to-air combat, a number of North Vietnamese MiGs falling victim to cannon-armed F-105 Thunderchiefs. Today, every new fighter carries a gun as standard. The Tomcat's Vulcan M61A1 20-mm cannon is installed to port, more or less below the front cockpit. Capable of a maximum rate of fire of 6,000rpm, it comes complete with 675 rounds of M50 ammunition and has the priceless advantage of being immune to modern-day countermeasures, the only effective defence being that of manoeuvre.

Below: Referred to in the accompanying text, this November 1973 test confirmed the ability of the Tomcat/Phoenix pairing when engaging multiple targets. Six missiles were launched in just 38 seconds at distances varying from 31 to 50 nautical miles, four of the drone targets being destroyed.

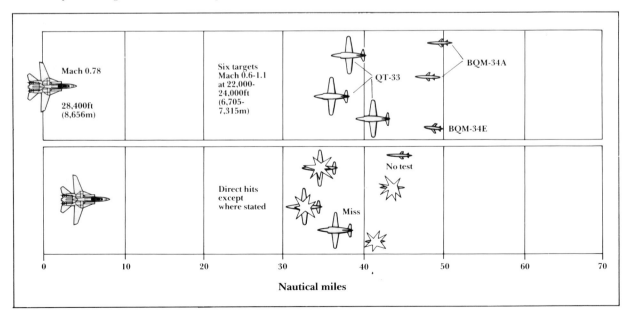

Above: This underside view of an F-14A on final approach for recovery aboard a Navy carrier clearly shows the main undercarriage housings beneath the fixed glove portion of the wing structure. Also in evidence are four Sparrow and four Sidewinder missiles plus two auxiliary fuel tanks.

Below: Underwing weapons stores stations may take either the AIM-7 Sparrow or AIM-54 Phoenix missile, shoulder fairings being suitable for use by the rather smaller and considerably lighter AIM-9 Sidewinder. In this picture, an AIM-7 is fitted beneath the wing of a development Tomcat.

Although originally developed with air-to-ground applications in mind, the F-14 has never been seriously viewed as a "mud-mover" and any aspirations it has in this direction are extremely modest to say the least, weaponry which could be employed being confined to conventional "iron bombs". Nevertheless, it does possess the ability to take a respectable payload—14,500lb (6,577kg) to be precise—and it is not beyond the realms of possibility that it could be pressed into use as a strike/close support fighter in a permissive environment. However, since such situations are likely to be few and far between, there seems to be little risk of Tomcat fighter jockeys being asked to compromise their much vaunted superiority by engaging in such mundane activities as merely dropping bombs or strafing ground targets.

By itself, of course, highly effective armament isn't

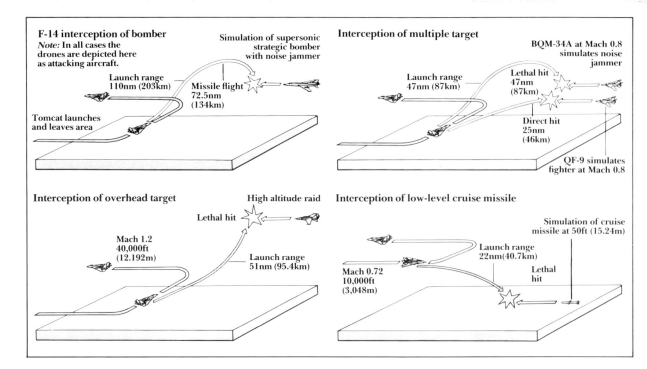

F-14 interception of bomber
Note: In all cases the drones are depicted here as attacking aircraft.

Simulation of supersonic strategic bomber with noise jammer

Launch range 110nm (203km)

Missile flight 72.5nm (134km)

Tomcat launches and leaves area

Interception of multiple target

BQM-34A at Mach 0.8 simulates noise jammer

Launch range 47nm (87km)

Lethal hit 47nm (87km)

Direct hit 25nm (46km)

QF-9 simulates fighter at Mach 0.8

Interception of overhead target

High altitude raid

Lethal hit

Mach 1.2 40,000ft (12.192m)

Launch range 51nm (95.4km)

Interception of low-level cruise missile

Simulation of cruise missile at 50ft (15.24m)

Launch range 22nm(40.7km)

Lethal hit

Mach 0.72 10,000ft (3,048m)

Above: Four of the types of interception likely to be accomplished by the F-14 Tomcat/AIM-54 Phoenix team are depicted here, all of these scenarios having been successfully evaluated in live firing trials utilising pilotless drone targets. That at top left resulted in the destruction of a BQM-34E drone simulating a "Backfire" type bomber flying at Mach 1.5 at 50,000ft (15,250m) while that at top right called for the F-14 to engage two targets, one of which was acting as a noise jammer to mask their approach. In the drawing above left a radar- augmented Bomarc target missile flying at Mach 2.8 at 72,000ft (21,950m) was engaged by a single Phoenix which passed well within lethal range while the final drawing (above right) portrays the effectiveness of Tomcat and Phoenix combination in an encounter with a small target like a cruise missile operating at low level (50ft/15m) and taking advantage of surface clutter. Although a direct hit did not result, the AIM-54 Phoenix again passed close enough to ensure destruction of the Firebee drone.

a great deal of use if one is unable to establish precisely where the enemy is, what he is doing and what degree of danger he represents. It is in precisely this area that the Tomcat scores heavily, since it does possess a remarkably sophisticated package of electronics which play an important part in enabling it to rank as one of the best fighters currently flying anywhere in the world, if not the best.

The AWG-9 radar

The Hughes Airborne Weapons Group Nine (AWG-9) weapon control system might be said to be the heart of the Tomcat; without it the F-14 would be good for little more than just dropping bombs and even that would require the assistance of "pathfinders" to pinpoint the target.

As its designation implies, AWG-9 is more than just a radar, other key component parts comprising a fire control system, a television sighting unit, cockpit display screens, two-way secure data link facilities and, almost inevitably, computers to process the vast array of data generated when working at full bore. Its origins predate those of the aircraft in which it is now installed for it too was conceived in the late '50s, initially in conjunction with the ill-fated Douglas F6D Missileer fighter, a project that was cancelled in 1960.

The avionics package survived, however, next being earmarked for the equally unfortunate F-111B. For AWG-9, it was definitely a case of third-time lucky; it outlived that disastrous episode and was selected for the F-14 in updated form with the ability to function with Sparrow and Sidewinder missiles as well as the Vulcan cannon. Despite gaining additional tasks along the way, the AWG-9 managed to shed a substantial amount of weight with the result that the system installed in the F-14 actually tipped the scales some 600lb (272.2kg) lighter that that of the F-111B.

The F-14's AWG-9 radar has a long range volume of cover about 15 times greater than that of the Tomcat's immediate predecessor, the F-4 Phantom.

Above: Wearing a helmet which features what appears to be VF-1 "Wolf Pack" insignia, a Hughes Aircraft Company engineer evaluates a new digital display unit being developed for the Tomcat's AN/AWG-9 weapons control system.

Below left: The Tomcat's front office is a mixture of ancient and modern technology, being dominated by the horizontal situation display that is partly obscured by the control column. Directly above is the vertical display.

Below right: The Radar Intercept Officer's cockpit differs markedly from that of the pilot, with perhaps the most notable feature being the circular tactical information display and the adjacent hand control stick.

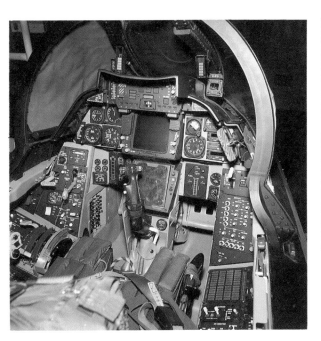

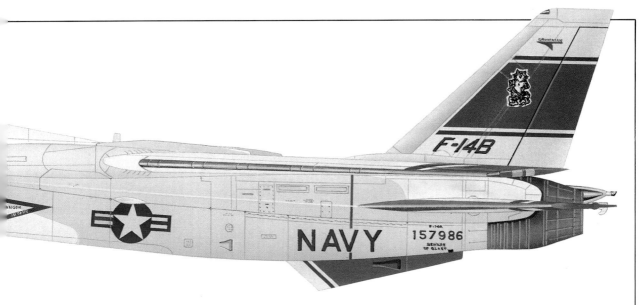

Above: The single example of the F-14B variant also ranks as being among the most attractive Tomcats. Still active today, 157986 is closely associated with F-14D development.

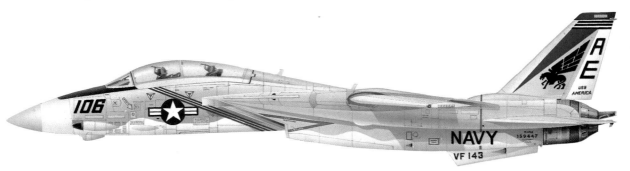

Above: Evidence of just how colourful some Tomcats were is provided by this example from VF-143 "Pukin' Dogs" while assigned to CVW-6 aboard the USS *America* in the late 1970s.

Left: The move to "low-viz" colours is evident in this plan view of a VF-143 Tomcat during the early 1980s. National insignia has been much reduced in size while the long-established practice of painting movable control surfaces, such as flaps, in white has been eliminated.

Below: Depicted in the colours it wore during service with the Naval Air Test Center at Patuxent River, Maryland, F-14A 158619 was destroyed when it crashed into the Chesapeake Bay while evaluating a variant of the original TF30 engine.

Left: Featuring all three types of missile armament, the VF-143 F-14A portrayed here is the subject of the plan view on page 26 and the side profile shown above.

Below: Comparison of this side view with that of the VF-143 machine on the previous page provides graphic confirmation of just how drastic was the move to "low-viz" markings.

Below: The latest front-line Navy fighter squadron to acquire the Tomcat, VF-154 has elected to retain markings very similar to those worn by the F-4 Phantom for many years.

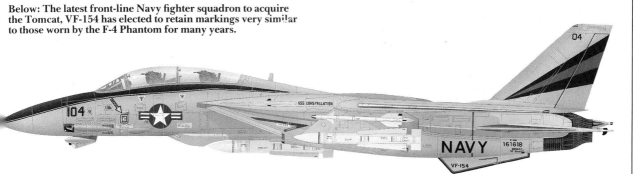

Below: Aircraft of VF-1, the first fully-operational Tomcat fighter unit, initially featured a most attractive scheme although this has given way to far less visible markings.

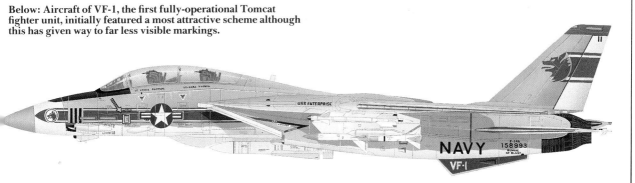

Below: Possibly the smartest Tomcats of all were those of VF-142 in the mid-to-late 1970s, the yellow and black trim being particularly well suited to Grumman's fighter.

Above: One of the most enduring examples of Navy unit insignia, VF-31's squadron badge features "Felix the Cat" and was still displayed on the F-14 until quite recently.

Above: The origins of VF-51's nickname "Screaming Eagles" are readily apparent when one studies the squadron badge which is not normally carried on the Tomcat.

Below: In view of the fact that they would mainly operate over desert, it was hardly surprising that Iran's F-14s were camouflaged, this basic pattern still being used today.

Below: Complete with Sukhoi "kill" symbol below the cockpit, Bu.No.160390 of VF-41 was one of the F-14As involved in the decisive encounter over the Gulf of Sidra in August 1981.

NAVY

F-14A
160390

Above: The first Navy fighter squadron to take delivery of the Tomcat was VF-124 at Miramar, their fairly nondescript insignia being depicted in this scrap view of the fin.

Above right: Also shore-based at Miramar, VF-211 "Checkmates" Tomcats were rather more handsome than those of VF-124, blue and red trim also appearing on the ventral fins.

3-863

BEWARE
OF BLAST

Left: Should the crew of an F-14 ever have to part company with their Tomcat in a hurry, the quickest way out is courtesy of Martin Baker's GRU-7A ejection seat which is fitted as standard in both front and rear cockpits.

Below: With facial features totally obscured by oxygen mask and sun visor, this self-portait of a VF-84 pilot at work in his "office" also conveys some idea of the excellent field of view bestowed by the Tomcat cockpit.

Above: The first US Navy Reserve fighter squadron to convert to the F-14A was Miramar-based VF-301 "Devil's Disciples" which began the transition in late 1984.

Above: Shore-based at Oceana, Virginia, VF-74 "Be-devilers" has recently been operating from the USS *Saratoga* with VF-103 as the fighter element of CVW-17.

Above: VF-213's unit badge features a cat of a rather different kind but one that is probably no less ferocious, hence the squadron nick-name "Black Lions".

AWG-9 incorporates second-generation solid state technology and, although primarily concerned with detecting, tracking and ranging of targets for the combined missile/gun armament, it can also function quite capably in air-to-ground modes. However, as noted elsewhere, air-to-ground does not form part of the Tomcat's operational brief and it is therefore not covered by the US Navy's training syllabus.

Perhaps the most important component is the 36in (91.4cm) planar-array radar scanner which has an effective range of about 150 miles (240km) and which can operate in three modes—search, track and

Above: One of the most important recent additions to the F-14 has been Northrop's AXX-1 Television Camera Set which permits targets to be identified well beyond "eyeball" range.

attack. Data pertaining to no fewer than two dozen targets may be handled at any given time, information on the developing tactical picture being conveyed to the Radar Intercept Officer (RIO) in the rear cockpit via a 12in (30.5cm) diameter video display unit (VDU).

Below: Continued updating of the Phoenix missile led to the appearance of the much-improved AIM-54C version, seen here being launched by a PMTC F-14 during early testing in 1980.

For detection at extreme ranges and in missile attacks employing the AIM-54 Phoenix, the radar operates in a pulsed-Doppler mode. For medium and short range engagements—such as those traditionally encountered in dogfighting—the conventional pulse mode is used and this can also provide continuous wave target illumination for the Sparrow missile which does, of course, require that the target be "painted" by radar if it is to home successfully.

Selecting the greatest threat

At ranges of about 100nm (185km), closure rates may be computed, details of these appearing with the direction of target travel and IFF data on the RIO's VDU. In addition, the weapons computer is able to allocate priority to specific targets on a closure basis, selecting those which appear to offer the greatest threat to the Tomcat's well-being or, for that matter, the Carrier Battle Group which the F-14 may be protecting.

Another AWG-9 function is that of vertical scan lock on, this being one of three modes of operation which may be employed in close combat. In vertical scan lock on, the radar antenna operates only in pitch, covering a fairly narrow cone and automatically locking on to targets within a five mile (8km) radius. Weapons launch information is presented to the pilot via the Kaiser Head-Up Display (HUD) and is continuously updated by computer in this and the other two "dogfight" modes, namely boresight and manual lock on.

Of all the AWG-9 modes, it is the track-while-scan

Below: Some idea of the quality of imagery offered by the Northrop TCS is evident in this picture of a Tomcat flying at ten times the range of the human eye.

facility which is the most remarkable, solely by virtue of being able to deal with 24 targets at once, although the work-load in such a situation could well exceed the capabilities of even the best trained crew, especially as a single aircraft would only be able to engage a small proportion of these. Of course, the system's computers help greatly in that they establish threat priorities, assign weapons to specific targets and notify the crew when the most desirable launch position is reached.

Other less spectacular AWG-9 functions include navigation, gun direction and air-to-ground computations, while it also possesses the now seemingly obligatory built-in test (BIT) facility, monitoring not only its own performance but also that of associated equipment, automatically notifying faults to the crew throughout the course of a mission.

Television Camera Sight

On early Tomcats, there was also a gimbal-mounted AN/ALR-23 infra-red detection set which could be coupled to the radar array or used independently to examine areas not being subjected to radar search. Unfortunately, this sensor sounded fine in theory but was by no means so satisfactory in reality and it was soon removed, giving way to the rather more useful Northrop AXX-1 Television Camera Sight (TCS), a device intended to permit positive

Above: Fitting snugly beneath the F-14's belly and containing optical and infra-red sensors, the Tactical Air Reconnaissance Pod System (TARPS) is now well established in Navy service.

identification of a potential target well outside "eyeball" range and one that has since been used for situations in which it is desirable to see before one can be seen.

The primary navigation aid is the AN/ASN-92(V) Carrier Aircraft Inertial Navigation System II (CAINS II) which comprises an AN/ASN-90 Inertial Measurement Unit (IMU), Litton's LC-728 navigation computer and associated equipment. IMU alignment normally takes five or six minutes and can be accomplished by radio-frequency data link, by deck-edge cable linking it with the parent carrier's Ship's Inertial Navigation System (SINS) or by a hand set. Appropriate controls and displays are provided for both crew members.

The Tomcat's Tactical Air Reconnaissance Pod System (TARPS) basically contains a mixture of cameras and infra-red linescanning sensors. It is viewed primarily as an interim reconnaissance system and is expected to remain operational until the dedicated RF-18 Hornet becomes available in a few years' time. Roughly 50 F-14As have been "wired" for TARPS, one of the two F-14A squadrons on each carrier usually operating three reconnaissance-configured aircraft alongside nine standard Tomcat fighters.

4

The Tomcat in Service

DESPITE the fact that it is a most complex machine, the interval between the Tomcat's maiden flight and its entry into service with elements of the US Navy was surprisingly short. Indeed, barely 21 months were to pass before, on 8 October 1972, the "Gunfighters" of VF-124 at NAS Miramar, California took delivery of their first F-14A, this effectively marking the start of the Tomcat's operational career.

In fact, although delivery of the first aircraft to VF-124 represented a high point in the process of transition from a fighter undergoing test to one capable of performing its designated operational tasking, the ceremonies at Miramar perhaps tended to obscure the fact that there was still plenty to be done before the Grumman fighter could begin to patrol the world's oceans effectively.

To be honest, VF-124's designation provides no real clue as to its precise role and the uninformed outsider could well be excused for believing that it is a fully operational unit. The reality is, however, rather different, VF-124 actually being one of a quite large number of Fleet Replacement Squadrons (FRSs) presently to be found in the US Navy line-up.

For many years now, this service has adopted what it describes as the "community concept" in which similarly-equipped units are concentrated at a single base within each of the two major Fleet organisations. Thus, for example, Atlantic Fleet light attack squadrons operating the A-7 Corsair are usually shore-based at NAS Cecil Field, Florida, while their Pacific Fleet equivalents use NAS Lemoore, California, as a home base when not deployed aboard an aircraft carrier. In the case of the fighter squadrons, the respective shore locations are NAS Oceana, Virginia and NAS Miramar.

Below: Cats, dogs and bears. Taken during the course of a 1983 NATO exercise over the North Atlantic, this photo shows a Soviet Tu-95 Bear boring onwards, seemingly oblivious to the close proximity of a trio of F-14A Tomcats from VF-143 "Pukin' Dogs" from the aircraft carrier USS *Dwight D. Eisenhower.*

Naturally, logistical considerations are greatly eased by using the single-base "community concept" but there are a number of other important benefits. For a start, putting all the squadrons engaged in a specific mission on just one base tends to encourage co-operation between units, the resulting cross-fertilization being of particular value with regard to disseminating tactical information. In addition, supporting units such as "aggressor" squadrons may also be assigned to a specific "community", close links of this kind greatly enhancing the benefit of the routine training which forms such an important part of the daily diet of operations when not at sea.

The remaining element invariably to be found in a specific "community" is the FRS. This can, in many ways, be viewed as a "parent" unit, for the FRS is now always the first Fleet element to take delivery of a new combat type, be it a helicopter, patrol aircraft or jet fighter. Once the initial cadre of instructors have familiarized themselves with the new type, they are responsible for drawing up a formal training syllabus and providing tuition in all aspects of the particular machine concerned for the air and ground crew who will ultimately operate it.

In addition, the FRS is tasked with managing the transition process and, eventually, when the type concerned is well established in service, for ensuring that there is a constant flow of fully-trained personnel to replace those being reassigned to other duty. Thus, although it may not be quite as glamorous as its "offspring", in that it is rarely called upon to act in an operational capacity, the Fleet Replacement Squadron is nevertheless a vital cog in today's naval aviation establishment.

This, then, was the task which faced VF-124, it being made slightly more complicated by the fact that the Navy decided to delay organizing an East Coast FRS until the F-14A was well established in service. As a result, VF-124 was initially responsible for managing the transition of a handful of Atlantic Fleet units as well as the Pacific Fleet squadrons that it would eventually "parent" on a permanent basis.

Deliveries slow

Although VF-124 took delivery of its first Tomcat in October 1972, the flow of aircraft from Grumman's facility at Calverton was slow to begin with. However, this was probably beneficial in that it permitted the pace of operations to be built up gradually. Not surprisingly, the "Gunfighter" personnel spent this early period mainly in becoming proficient on the new fighter and in drawing up the formal training syllabus.

Below: The skull and crossbones motif on the fin of these two Tomcats helps to identify them as being assigned to VF-84 "Jolly Rogers". In conjunction with sister squadron VF-41—the famed "Sukhoi-killers"—VF-84 has operated as part of Carrier Air Wing Eight since receiving the F-14 in 1976.

By the spring of 1973, VF-124 had received sufficient aircraft to begin training aircrews earmarked for assignment to the first operational units. These, too, formed part of the Pacific Fleet's Fighter and Airborne Early Warning Wing (FitAEWWing), both having been formally commissioned at Miramar during October 1972.

The two squadrons concerned—VF-1 "Wolf Pack" and VF-2 "Bounty Hunters"—would eventually share the distinction of introducing Tomcat to seagoing service, but that lay a long way off in the future when they began training under VF-124's careful eyes. By July 1973, they had progressed sufficiently far along the transition path to begin to take delivery of their own aircraft although neither squadron received a full complement of 12 Tomcats until March of the following year.

Then, the previously demanding level of activity intensified as both squadrons set about a hectic training schedule which culminated in their being declared combat-ready, this work-up period being highlighted by a successful operational readiness inspection (ORI) which gave the green light for the first extended period of sea duty.

Tomcat's maiden deployment was made aboard the USS *Enterprise* (CVAN-65), then unique in being the US Navy's only nuclear-powered aircraft carrier and a fitting vessel to introduce the newest fighter to the combat inventory. Home-ported at Alameda, just a few miles from San Francisco, *Enterprise* would deploy with elements of Carrier Air Wing 14 (CVW-14), final preparations for the cruise beginning in mid-September when VF-1 and VF-2 each flew a dozen aircraft north from Miramar to the Naval Air Station which lies adjacent to the naval dockyard. Once there, the aircrews turned their mounts over to the loading teams which wasted little time in hoisting the costly fighters aboard by crane, an undignified way in which to begin a long voyage but one which is standard Navy operating procedure.

Eventually, with all the 80 or so aircraft that made up CVW-14's cutting edge safely aboard, *Enterprise* slipped her moorings and set course for the distant Western Pacific on 17 September 1974 at the start of an eventful eight-month cruise. As far as the two Tomcat squadrons were concerned, the tour was quite successful in that it featured a number of live firing exercises in which examples of all three types of missile armament were expended, while both squadrons also flew combat air patrol (CAP) missions over Saigon during the final stages of the American evacuation.

Below: "Black Aces" meet "Black Panther". A brace of Tomcats from VF-41 aboard the USS *Nimitz* desert their CAP station for a few moments to take on fuel from a KA-6D Intruder of VA-35. Both of the F-14s are carrying Phoenix missiles beneath the fuselage but no other armament is apparent.

On the debit side, flight crew faced a period of enforced inactivity when the Tomcat was temporarily grounded following the loss of a couple of aircraft during January 1975. Both victims were from VF-1 and both incidents were apparently caused by fan blade failure culminating in fire. Fortunately, all four crew members were recovered safely after rapidly parting company with the stricken aircraft, their spirits being literally and metaphorically dampened by an unplanned dip in the South China Sea.

Above: Trio from Miramar: Tomcats from VF-1 (leading), VF-2 (nearest camera) and VF-51 take time out for a bit of loose formation flying over the Pacific Ocean during 1982.

Atlantic and Mediterranean deployment

On balance, though, the maiden cruise was viewed as a great success, the two squadrons accumulating a combined total of close to 3,000 flying hours by the time they returned to Miramar in the latter half of May 1975. The focus of attention then switched to the Atlantic Fleet which was on the verge of making its first Tomcat deployment, the two squadrons concerned—VF-14 "Tophatters" and VF-32 "Swordsmen"—having completed transition training with VF-124 at Miramar in 1974 while VF-1 and VF-2 entered the terminal stages of preparation to deploy.

Returning to Oceana in the late summer of 1974, VF-14 and VF-32 spent much of the next nine months honing their skills in anticipation of intro-ducing Grumman's newest "cat" to service with the 6th Fleet in the Mediterranean. This tour of duty eventually kicked-off with departure from Norfolk, Virginia on 28 June 1975 and was, if anything, rather more successful than the Tomcat's first cruise.

Assigned to CVW-1 and operating from the USS *John F. Kennedy* (CV-67), the two squadrons spent some seven months away from home, taking part in a succession of NATO-sponsored manoeuvres as well as flexing their claws against the French Air Force

Below: A Sidewinder- and Sparrow-armed Tomcat of VF-74 taxies clear of the arrester wire after recovering aboard the USS *Saratoga* (CV-60) of the 6th Fleet during flight operations off Libya early in 1986, before the USAF's F-111s joined USN aircraft in reprisal attacks on Libyan mainland targets, in April.

(FAF) in "Exercise Lafayette" when FAF Mirage IIIs and Jaguar As made repeated attempts to penetrate the fighter screen around the Carrier Battle Group. Eventually, no fewer than 91 sorties were recorded by the French, all of which were successfully intercepted by Tomcats from *Kennedy* working in concert with another Grumman product, namely the E-2C Hawkeye AEW platform.

Although the engine-related problems which were beginning to give rise to great concern had some impact on the number of Tomcats in commission at any time, both squadrons appeared to have met or exceeded most of their obligations without too much difficulty and they did at least manage to complete the tour without losing any aircraft to engine failure, the only casualty being a VF-14 Tomcat which ran off the flight deck when an arrester gear wire snapped at an unfortunate moment.

Tomcats and Beirut evacuation

Two more Atlantic Fleet squadrons—VF-142 "Ghost Riders" and VF-143 "Pukin' Dogs"—followed VF-14 and VF-32 through VF-124's "Tomcat School" at Miramar in the latter part of 1974 and, once again, there was a long interval between re-equipping and returning to sea duty. Initially attached to CVW-8, it was not until April 1976 that VF-142 and VF-143 headed eastbound for the Mediterranean and duty with the 6th Fleet. By then,

Above: Resplendent in high-visibility unit insignia, national markings and the like, this aircraft took part in VF-14's first F-14 cruise aboard the USS John F. Kennedy in 1975-76.

they had been reassigned to CVW-6 which embarked aboard the USS *America* (CV-66) for a six-month cruise highlighted by "Operation Fluid Drive" in late July when Tomcats of both squadrons furnished CAP cover for the evacuation of just over 300 civilians from Beirut which, even then, was being ravaged by civil war.

Even as VF-142 and VF-143 were working up to fully-operational status, steps were in hand to ease the burden on VF-124 which was still the only Tomcat FRS and which was hard-pressed to satisfy the needs of both major Fleets. Accordingly, in the autumn of 1975, the Oceana-based F-4 Phantom FRS began to take delivery of the F-14 in anticipation of assuming responsibility for supporting Atlantic Fleet fighter squadrons equipped with or destined to receive the Tomcat.

The unit concerned was VF-101—colloquially known as the "Grim Reapers"—and for a time it continued to serve as a dual-type FRS with both the F-4 and the F-14 before the Phantom-equipped element split away to provide a basis for VF-171 in August 1977. Not surprisingly, VF-124 furnished a considerable amount of assistance to VF-101 which wasted little time in initiating its own transition programme, VF-41 "Black Aces" and VF-84 "Jolly Rogers" being the first two squadrons to convert at

Oceana, a task which was successfully accomplished in the summer of 1976.

Thereafter, the flow of new-build Tomcats reaching the Navy entered a period of decline and, with most being earmarked to re-equip Pacific Fleet squadrons, VF-101 was not called upon to manage any more transition programmes until the summer of 1980 when VF-11 and VF-31 converted from the Phantom.

Over on the West Coast, though, VF-124 had been hard at work and, with its obligations to the Atlantic Fleet at an end, it reverted to furnishing support for Pacific Fleet echelons, a task which began in the summer of 1975 when VF-24 "Fighting Renegades" and VF-211 "Fighting Checkmates" both picked up the F-14. These two squadrons returned to sea duty as part of CVW-9 aboard the USS *Constellation* (CV-64) in April 1977.

Barely had they completed the formal tuition process when VF-124 welcomed its next intake of students, these being destined to join VF-114 "Aardvarks" and VF-213 "Black Lions" aboard the USS *Kitty Hawk* (CV-63) as part of CVW-11. Both squadrons turned in the F-4J Phantom for the F-14A during the early part of 1976 but, once again, some 18 months were to pass before they went back to sea, embarking for their first Tomcat cruise in October 1977.

VF-124 then enjoyed a well-earned respite from the task of managing transition, almost two years

Above: Close formation of VF-211 "Flying Checkmates" Tomcats operating from USS *Constellation*. Note Sidewinder and Sparrow armament on two nearest aircraft only.

being allowed to slip by before VF-51 "Screaming Eagles" and VF-111 "Sundowners" reported to the classroom in early 1978 to begin conversion from the veteran F-4N Phantom to Grumman's rather more sophisticated machine. In the event, these two units made their maiden F-14 deployment aboard the USS *Kitty Hawk* as part of CVW-15 between May 1979 and February 1980.

Reserve squadrons convert

Since then, VF-124 has assisted in the transition of the last two Pacific Fleet front-line fighter squadrons scheduled to acquire the F-14, these being VF-21 "Freelancers" and VF-154 "Black Knights", a process which began in November 1983. Completion of that phase of the re-equipment programme did not, however, mark the end of VF-124's involvement in this line of work for it was also instrumental in assisting the two Miramar-based Naval Air Reserve Force fighter squadrons to convert from the F-4S Phantom to the F-14A. The two units involved—VF-301 "Devil's Disciples" and VF-302 "Stallions"—successfully accomplished the lengthy job of re-equipment during 1984-85, conversion being complicated by the fact that, since they are mainly manned by reservists, the training process was of necessity rather longer than that of a regular Fleet fighter squadron.

At Oceana in the meantime, VF-101 resumed transition activity in the summer of 1980 when VF-11 "Red Rippers" and VF-31 "Tomcatters" both received the F-14 with which they eventually deployed as part of CVW-3 aboard the USS *John F. Kennedy* in January 1982. VF-33 "Tarsiers" and VF-102 "Diamondbacks" followed suit in the summer of 1981, joining CVW-1 on the USS *America* for their maiden full-length F-14 cruise in early December 1982, although they had completed a successful two-month "mini-deployment" for a NATO exercise in the late summer of that year.

Tomcats shoot down Fitters

Exercises are intended to ensure readiness of aircraft and crew in the event of the "real thing" ever happening. It did just that for two Tomcats in a somewhat unexpected manner when, in the space of a few furious seconds over the Gulf of Sidra (which Colonel Gaddaffi had claimed as Libyan territory) on 19 August 1981, they demonstrated emphatically that the F-14 is not an adversary to tangle with.

On that date, two Libyan Arab Republic Air Force (LARAF) Sukhoi Su-22 Fitter-Js were foolhardy enough to take on two F-14As of VF-41 "Black Aces" from the USS *Nimitz* (CVN-68). One of the LARAF fighters launched a single Atoll heat-seeking missile as the opposing pairs of aircraft converged but this failed to guide, hardly surprisingly since it was launched well outside what is considered to be the weapon's envelope. Nevertheless, the rules of engagement laid down for the US Navy pilots meant that they were now in the position of being able to return fire if they chose to do so.

Retribution was indeed swift in coming and proved deadly for one of the hapless Libyan pilots. Each Tomcat engaged a Fitter, and both Fitters were despatched quite efficiently in an encounter which was particularly economical in terms of weaponry expended. One AIM-9L Sidewinder was launched by each F-14, these homing accurately on their respective targets. Although both Fitter pilots were seen to eject, only one parachute canopy was observed, which indicates that one Libyan paid the supreme penalty.

Replacing the last Phantoms

Re-equipment of Atlantic Fleet fighter squadrons was concluded in 1983 when the last two units—VF-74 "Bedevilers" and VF-103 "Sluggers"—relinquished the Phantom. As was usual practice, their return to front-line status took some time and it

Below: In the more ordered calm of a briefing room aboard the USS *Nimitz*, Cdr Henry Kleeman and Lt David Venlet relive their few brief moments of "high anxiety" over the Gulf of Sidra as they relate their part in the destruction of two Libyan Su-22 Fitters on 19 August 1981.

was not until April 1984 that they set course for the Mediterranean as part of CVW-17 on the recently overhauled USS *Saratoga* (CV-60).

Export Tomcats

As far as export customers are concerned, the Tomcat hasn't exactly set the world on fire. Only Iran has opted to buy Grumman's fighter in the 15 years which have passed since it first flew. Nevertheless, the Iranian sale was significant, for it was instrumental in helping Grumman to remain afloat during a period of grave financial worries.

The Iranian decision to purchase the Tomcat was reached in August 1973 and was in part prompted by a desire to do something about Soviet MiG-25 Foxbat reconnaissance aircraft which had been regularly overflying Iran, immune from interception. Discussion between President Nixon and the Shah in 1972 cleared the way for the Iranian order but US Government approval was not forthcoming until November 1973. Eventually, a total of 80 Tomcats was ordered, in two separate batches. The first contract, calling for 30 aircraft, was signed in January 1974, 50 more being the subject of a further order placed in the following June. Flying for the first time in the latter half of 1975, deliveries got under way with an initial batch of three aircraft which arrived at Teheran (Mehrabad) air base on 27 January 1976. By July 1978, 76 more examples had followed, one

Tomcat being retained in the USA as a test specimen; this is now apparently in long-term store following the departure of the Shah in 1979, the establishment of a new regime and the subsequent breakdown in US-Iranian relations.

At the time that the F-14 entered service, Grumman had several hundred personnel in Iran to furnish support and it is probable that serviceability was high. With the revolution, though, Grumman hastily and wisely withdrew from the country and the number of aircraft in commission almost certainly plummeted sharply, partly due to the non-availability of spares and partly to inadequate maintenance, for it is generally accepted that Iranian technicians lack the skill of Grumman's.

More recently, however, it appears that the renamed Islamic Republic of Iran Air Force (IRIAF) has succeeded in restoring a number of aircraft to airworthy condition, there being persistent reports that the Tomcat has been used quite extensively in the long and bloody war with neighbouring Iraq. Whether or not these are able to call upon the full capability of the Hughes AWG-9 and its associated weaponry is not known, but in view of repeated Iraqi claims to have downed Tomcats in air-to-air combat it seems highly unlikely.

Below: Framed in the cockpit of a seventh aircraft, six Iranian Air Force Tomcats fly in loose formation over the desert. Today, such a scene would probably be difficult to recreate. These were among 79 supplied to the "previous management", and some are said to have seen action against Iraq.

5
Future Tomcats

UNLIKE its contemporaries, Tomcat has changed little since it entered operational service, a fact which says a lot for the "rightness" of the design. However, the F-14's evolution has certainly been fraught with problems.

For a start, the TF30 engine was originally intended to be an interim powerplant and the fact that this became the "definitive" engine may well have been a result of the American withdrawal from Vietnam. A period of retrenchment followed that conflict, this being marked by relative "austerity" with regard to military matters, it no longer being possible to resolve problems by throwing money at them until they went away.

As a result, the Navy had to persevere with the F-14A, the embarrassing engine-related problems being a major factor in the high attrition experienced during the latter half of the 1970s which eventually forced adoption of a more reliable powerplant.

At the same time, it was also evident that the AWG-9 was beginning to show signs of age and vulnerability in the face of rapidly-improving Soviet ECM expertise. It was thus decided that any major effort at enhancing Tomcat should also encompass improvements to the weapon control system.

Development of the F-14D

To accomplish these disparate objectives, Grumman was awarded an $864 million contract in summer 1984 for development of the F-14D which will feature the long-overdue "new" engine as well as revised avionics and radar.

Re-engining of the Tomcat is by no means a new idea, the Pratt & Whitney F401-powered F-14B having been evaluated in 1973-74 before being abandoned in a cost-cutting exercise. This idea then lapsed until the late 1970s when all three of the leading American engine manufacturers were actively pursuing the development of new powerplants.

Once again, though, lack of funds killed off this attempt and it was not until early in the 1980s that any progress was made. Even then, events moved slowly despite promising early trials with the F101DFE (derivative fighter engine).

Ground and air tests

Based on General Electric's F101 which had been chosen for the Rockwell B-1, the F101DFE began life rather tentatively, just five test engines being involved, the first two of which were designated F101-X. With ground running successfully negotiated, the focus shifted to airborne evaluation, the sole F-14B being fitted with a pair of the new engines in the first half of 1981.

Referred to by Grumman as the "Super Tomcat", the revamped F-14B resumed flight operations on 14 July 1981, logging some 50 flights and 70 hours between then and the spring of 1982. This testing soon revealed that the F101DFE bestowed significant performance benefits throughout the envelope, some idea of its potential being given by the fact that loiter time in the combat air patrol mission rose by no less than 34 per cent.

The ensuing evaluation of test-generated data led to the decision to proceed with full-scale development of the F101DFE as the F110 in October 1982. However, the Navy remained cautious, opting to monitor Pratt & Whitney's PW1128N which also seemed to possess some potential as a TF30 replacement. In the event, the US Air Force probably forced the Navy's hand when, on 3 February 1984, it selected the F110 to power both the F-15 and F-16. Four days later, the Navy followed suit, announcing that the F110-GE-400 would be installed in production Tomcats from 1988 onwards.

In broad terms, the F110-GE-400 differs little from the USAF's dash 100 version although, inevitably, some modification is necessary in order for it to fit Tomcat. The most visible evidence of this concerns the area between the main body of the engine and the afterburner, a 50in (1.27m) section being inserted to eliminate the need for costly modifications to the air inlet system. Inlet ramp scheduling will, however, require some revision, while other less obvious changes concern the gearbox and a few other components which have had to be relocated.

With a maximum augmented thrust rating of some 27,080lb (12,283kg), the F110-GE-400 is significantly more powerful than the existing TF30-P-414A, while it is also much less thirsty in afterburner. No less welcome is the prospect of greater durability, for the F110 hot-section inspection life of 1,500 hours greatly exceeds the TF30's 880-hour figure.

Flight testing of the F110 in the Tomcat was expected to begin in summer 1986 with the F-14B/F101DFE test-bed being resurrected yet again to verify engine performance and expand the envelope. Of the four other Tomcats that will be most closely associated with F-14D development, only one will be fitted with F110 engines, this (Bu.No.161867) being known in company parlance as PA-2. Expected to fly in March 1987, PA-2 will also carry the new avionics and radar and can thus be said to be a true F-14D prototype. PA-2's initial function will be that of an engine test-bed to clear the way for the F110-powered F-14A(Plus) which is due to enter service in spring 1988. Thereafter, it will join three other Tomcats in avionics and radar testing.

Airborne evaluation of the radar is to begin in February 1987 aboard a Douglas TA-3B Skywarrior. As previously noted, PA-2 will have a part to play but the main burden will initially fall on three TF30-engined Tomcats referred to by Grumman as PA-1, PA-3 and PA-4. PA-1 (Bu.No.161865) is to fly first, shortly before PA-2, and will begin by checking out

Below: Employed to test the General Electric F101DFE, the F-14B prototype was renamed "Super Tomcat" by Grumman, a name which failed to find favour with the US Navy.

navigation functions as well as basic system testing. The main job of PA-3 (Bu.No.162589), which is expected to fly for the first time in summer 1987, will be radar development while PA-4 (either Bu.No.161623 or 161624) will concentrate on weapons and stores management. This aircraft is also due to make its maiden flight in summer 1987.

With Grumman being asked to satisfy certain Navy requirements as the programme progresses, it has been decided to adopt an incremental approach in developing radar and associated equipment. Thus, no less than seven sets of software tapes will be used so as to "make haste slowly", additional functions being incorporated as testing moves ahead. The first set (G1) will be installed only in the TA-3B, all of the Tomcats involved starting with G2. Thereafter, sets G3 to G7 will join the programme at set intervals between mid-1987 and early 1989. The definitive version, G7, will be fitted to production-configured F-14Ds. In the meantime, formal Navy operational test and evaulation will take place in 1989, clearing the way for Fleet introduction in 1990.

New, more secure radar

Without doubt the key feature of the F-14D will be the new radar, presently being referred to simply as APG-XX. In reality, it will basically be an updated version of the AWG-9, incorporating recent advances in digital technology, micro-miniaturization and "hardening" to render it less vulnerable to enemy ECM.

As far as APG-XX capability is concerned, the switch to monopulse angle tracking enables target location to be pinpointed within the radar beam, this contributing greatly to the raid assessment mode in which individual aircraft operating in close formation may be detected. Digital scan control permits better management of antenna scan pattern, most notably in track-while-scan (TWS) mode when it permits a form of "time-sharing", enabling APG-XX to observe other likely areas of interest. Thus, it is not vulnerable to what might be described as "tunnel vision", in which one contact is concentrated on to the exclusion of everything else.

One particularly novel feature concerns target identification; APG-XX permits this to be accomplished by analysis of radar returns, with associated software presumably including a "library" of radar

Above: From underneath, the "Super Tomcat" doesn't look all that different, most of the changes that were made being buried well out of sight beneath the aircraft's skin.

footprints for comparison. As well as being generally a much more capable radar, APG-XX will possess far greater resistance to ECM. In the past, the AWG-9's great strength has permitted it to "burn through" ECM, but potential enemies are now turning to highly sophisticated electronic deception with which the F-14A/AWG-9 pairing is increasingly less able to deal. The F-14D's ECCM (electronic counter-countermeasures) "hardening" includes low-sidelobe antenna and side lobe-blanking guard channel, frequency agility and a digital programmable signal processor. The latter is actually inherited from the same company's AN/APG-70 radar set, itself just one element of the F-15 Eagle multi-stage improvement programme (MSIP). Other elements "lifted" from the APG-70 include an analogue signal converter to digitize information from the radar receiver, as well as the radar data processor which marries target data generated by the programmable signal processor with other information to solve tracking equations.

Of course, all of this data isn't much use without adequate management and distribution. On the F-14D, five data buses will direct sensor-generated information to the correct destination for processing. Two are mission buses, operating purely in support of avionics while there is also an interprocessor or computer bus, a radar bus and an armament bus.

Above: A General Dynamics Pomona proposal for a Phoenix replacement, the AMS (Advanced Missile System), depicted firing tandem-boosted missiles from a retractable box and including wing-mounted look-down shoot-down radar.

Coding of data will ensure that information gets to where it is likely to be of most value and, despite its apparent complexity, the entire transfer system is less complicated than that of the F-14A.

Computers also have an important part to play on the F-14D itself, each of the two avionics mission buses being linked with its own Cubic Corporation AN/AYK-14 unit. The computers are, in turn, linked by the interprocessor bus to the radar data processor and the radar intercept officer's digital display, which is itself also new. Numerous measures have been built into the package in order to elminate as far as possible the likelihood of failure or the need for degraded-system operation.

Cockpit displays simpler

To ease the high work-load, the cockpit has also been redesigned, most work of this nature being directed towards presenting tactical information in a more easily comprehended format. Not surprisingly, new digital technology features prominently; the front cockpit is now dominated by three multi-function cathode ray tubes identical to those of the F-18 Hornet. Data presented on these concerns the vertical situation, the horizontal situation and electronic warfare "threats", while the head-up display (HUD) is also the subject of some improvements. Turning to the rear cockpit, the predominant feature is the new radar digital display but this work station will also incorporate the existing F-14A tactical information display plus CRTs to present data relating to the horizontal situation and electronic warfare.

Self-protection jammer

Several Pentagon-sponsored items of equipment will also appear on the F-14D. Top of the list is the ITT/Westinghouse AN/ALQ-165 airborne self-protection jammer (ASPJ). Equally effective against pulsed or continuous wave radars, it may operate in either deception or noise jamming modes and is reported to be far superior to the F-14A's present equipment. Unfortunately, cost overruns and technical difficulties have delayed deployment.

On the F-14D, ASPJ will be built-in but the older F-14A will have to carry it in an external pod, possibly with some penalty in terms of weapons payload. In addition to ASPJ, other Pentagon-inspired equipment will include a new infra-red search and track sensor (IRST) and the joint tactical information distribution system (JTIDS). The former is presently under development by both General Electric and ITT who are engaged in a competitive programme.

The IRST will be located beneath the nose section

alongside Northrop's television camera sight.

Also still in the development phase, JTIDS is a jam-resistant two-way data link facility which permits rapid and secure transfer of information pertaining to friendly forces as well as enemy tracks and positions, command data, weather and digitized voice. Tomcat is expected to use Class 2 equipment which, while less complex and costly than that due for installation in command posts and airborne early warning platforms, can hardly be described as "cheap". Indeed, each F-14D JTIDS terminal is likely to cost around $200,000, providing graphic confirmation that updating Tomcat is by no means an exercise in economy.

APPENDIX I: F-14A TOMCAT SPECIFICATION DATA

Dimensions
Length: 62ft 10.6in (19.10m)
Span: 64ft 1.5in (19.55m) wings spread
38ft 2.4in (11.65m) wings at full sweep
33ft 3.5in (10.15m) wings overswept for stowage
Gross wing area: 565 sq ft (52,49m2)
Aspect ratio: 7.28 unswept
Height: 16ft 0in (4.88m)

Weights
Empty: 39,921lb (18,108kg)
Normal take-off: 58,571lb (26,567kg)
Maximum take-off: 74,349lb (33,724kg)

Engines/Fuel Capacity
Two Pratt & Whitney TF30-P-414A turbofans, each rated at 20,900lbst (9,480kg) in afterburner.
Internal fuel: 16,200lb (7,348kg)
External fuel: 3,784lb (1,716kg)

Performance
Vmax (clean): Mach 2.34 at 40,000ft (12,190m)
Patrol cruise speed: 400–550kt (741–1,019km/h)
Sea level climb rate: 30,000ft/min (9,140m/min)
Service ceiling: 56,000ft (17,070m)
Maximum range: 1,740nm (3,220km)

Armament One General Electric M61A1 Vulcan 20mm rotary cannon with 675 rounds of ammunition plus various combinations of AIM-7 Sparrow, AIM-9 Sidewinder and AIM-54 Phoenix air-to-air missiles. Typical loads include four AIM-54, two AIM-7 and two AIM-9 or six AIM-54 and two AIM-9.

APPENDIX II: F-14A TOMCAT PRODUCTION LIST

Variant	Serial Numbers	Variant	Serial Numbers	Variant	Serial Numbers
F-14A-01-GR	157980	F-14A-55-GR	157991	F-14A-100-GR	160652-160696
F-14A-05-GR	157981	F-14A-60-GR	158612-158619	F-14A-105-GR	160887-160930
F-14A-10-GR	157982	F-14A-65-GR	158620-158637	F-14A-110-GR	161133-161168
F-14A-15-GR	157983	F-14A-70-GR	158978-159006	F-14A-115-GR	161270-161299
F-14A-20-GR	157984	F-14A-75-GR	159007-159025	F-14A-120-GR	161416-161445
F-14A-25-GR	157985	F-14A-75-GR	159421-159429	F-14A-125-GR	161597-161626
F-14A-30-GR	157986	F-14A-80-GR	159430-159468	F-14A-130-GR	161850-161873
F-14A-35-GR	157987	F-14A-85-GR	159588-159637	F-14A-135-GR	162588-162611
F-14A-40-GR	157988	F-14A-90-GR	159825-159874	F-14A-140-GR	162688-162711
F-14A-45-GR	157989	F-14A-GR	160299-160378*		
F-14A-50-GR	157990	F-14A-95-GR	160379-160414		

*Aircraft with serial numbers 160299-160378 were supplied to Iran, 160299-328 being equivalent to Navy Block 90, remainder equivalent to Navy Block 95.

APPENDIX III: F-14A TOMCAT SQUADRONS OF THE US NAVY

Fighter Wing One, NAS Oceana, Va.
VF-11 Red Rippers
VF-14 Tophatters
VF-31 Tomcatters
VF-32 Swordsmen
VF-33 Tarsiers
VF-41 Black Aces
VF-74 Be-devilers
VF-84 Jolly Rogers
VF-101 Grim Reapers (FRS)
VF-102 Diamondbacks
VF-103 Sluggers
VF-142 Ghostriders
VF-143 Pukin' Dogs

Fighter and Airborne Early Warning Wing Pacific, NAS Miramar, Ca.
VF-1 Wolf Pack
VF-2 Bounty Hunters
VF-21 Freelancers
VF-24 Fighting Renegades
VF-51 Screaming Eagles
VF-111 Sundowners
VF-114 Aardvarks
VF-124 Gunfighters (FRS)
VF-154 Black Knights
VF-211 Fighting Checkmates
VF-213 Black Lions

Naval Air Reserve Force
VF-301 Devil's Disciples
VF-302 Stallions
(Note: both units operate from NAS Miramar, Ca.)

Other Operators
VX-4 Evaluators — NAS Point Mugu, Ca.
NATC/SATD — NAS Patuxent River, Md.
PMTC — NAS Point Mugu, Ca.
NASA Dryden — Edwards AFB, Ca.

PRINTED IN BELGIUM BY

proost
INTERNATIONAL BOOK PRODUCTION